The Lost Spring

Persephone did not
come back from the underworld,
Spring Maiden did not
bring spring to us this year.
I look, I search all over for her;
I scramble, I strive,
I run and run

and keep on running....
like Forrest Gump,
as though there's no tomorrow.

I wrote one villanelle
per day since 3/16/2020
before shelter-in-place
was announced in the San
Francisco Bay Area, California.

And this morning (5/4/2020):

I stop running,
take a breath,
and discover,
I did not end up
at the end of the world.

Planet earth is still here.
I can take a walk.

An Invitation

Join me for a walk.

You are invited.

Be it 6 feet apart, 60 feet......6 miles, 60 miles.....6,000 miles.... wherever you are.

This pandemic is a world-wide tragedy of historical proportions.

Although no one suffers or experiences this trauma the same way, we probably all felt some degree of shock, frustration, stress, setback, victimization, disgust, being beaten down, helplessness, harrowing, turmoil, animus.....

At the same time, unfortunately, we witnessed deaths and the picture of what death is like; tears, blame, lament, depression, hopelessness, a glimmer of hope......

In addition, we also try to grasp a prescient glimpse of our future, to salvage a dream, to go back to normal and a desire to heal.

It will be a long strife; in the end, it may take more than a vaccine, or another vacation and dining out to salve our wounds.

We need a way to make sense out of this calamitous catastrophe.

Then, poetry arrives.

These poems are my diary to reflect the day-to-day headlines, debates, emotions....

It is a tiny, humble reaction to the ongoing debacles.

I chose an ancient form of villanelle to compose these poems, to parallel the plagues that have been with us over centuries of archaic human history.

The majority of the poems follow similar structure and some or all rhyming schemes of villanelle.

Persephone's Spring

Poems by Livingston Rossmoor

Published by
EGW Publishing
(Since 1979)

Poetry Books by Livingston Rossmoor*

A Stream Keeps Running (2013)

Do You Hear What I Sing (2014)

A Journey in the Animal Kingdom (2014)

A Never-Ending Battle (2015)

When Ruby was Still in My Arms (2015)

I Hear the Ocean Landing (2016)

The Thunder Was So Mad (2017)

I Found Ruth Tonight (2017)

Collected Triplets (2018)

Selected Ballads, Villanelles, Couplets,
Tanka Sequences, Cinquains & Triplets (2018)

Selected Sonnets (2018)

Selected Poems 2002-2017 (2018)

Heart's Thread (2020)

Persephone's Spring (2020)

*For details, please visit www.livingstonrossmoor.com

Also by Livingston Rossmoor

Old Buddy Chang (2001)
(13 short stories)

One Ray of Light at Dawn (2002)
(poetry & prose)

DVD & CD-One Ray of Light at Dawn (2003)
(12 Lyrics & Melodies)

One Ray of Light at Dawn (2005)
(Book of Music Scores)

The Beauty and the Ugly (2006)
(poetry & prose)

DVD-Perpetual Stream (2007)
(10 Lyrics & Melodies)

Perpetual Stream (2009)
(Book of Music Scores)

I dedicate this book to all of the courageous
Essential Frontline Workers who continue
to work tirelessly during this pandemic.

Thanks to Lisa Rigge, Charles Sandler,
Andy Shinkle and Chris Slaughter for
reviewing this book. I also wish to thank
Chris Slaughter for the organization
and production of this book.

EGW Publishing (since 1979)

ISBN: 978-0-916393-46-5

www.livingstonrossmoor.com

TABLE OF CONTENTS

There is poetry as soon as we realize we possess nothing.

John Cage

I
The Gravity

The Gravity (3/16/2020)

This invisible thing is everywhere,
it ignores our arrogance, like gravity.
Rich, poor, nobodies, dignitaries, no one spared.

Bitsy virus forces us rethink what we are:
our life, values, faith, eternity and brevity.
This invisible thing is everywhere.

It pulls us down, forces us to swallow our tears,
fight as one, disregard malice and enmity.
Rich, poor, nobodies, dignitaries, no one spared.

It makes us humble, so much unknown and fear.
When will it end? How to keep our sanity?
This invisible thing is everywhere.

It lives on surfaces, it hangs in the air.
Probe, test, find a way to earn back our dignity.
Rich, poor, nobodies, dignitaries, no one spared.

Human limits are being pushed to the core;
nerve, guts, audacity, ingenuity...
This invisible thing is everywhere.
Rich, poor, nobodies, dignitaries, no one spared.

Still No Testing Kits (3/17/2020)

Yes, basement's all infested, the rat, the rat.
How bad? Why can't we turn the lights on?
Why refuse to wear glasses? Blind as a bat.

Layoffs, no work, no place to hang a hat.
Breadlines, soup kitchens, a memory long gone.
Yes, basement's all infested, the rat, the rat.

Isolate, duck to become just a stat.
Abide, stick to guidelines, use brains, not brawn.
Why refuse to wear glasses? Blind as a bat.

Look into the future, strain not a gnat.
Rain, storms, truth, lies, a new world will dawn.
Yes, basement's all infested, the rat, the rat.

Flatten the curve, everyday life is flat.
Sky is not falling, moon still up, but stars are wan.
Why refuse to wear glasses? Blind as a bat.

Invisible enemy stares at us while we spat,
debate how the gory battle can be won?
Yes, basement's all infested, the rat, the rat.
Why refuse to wear glasses? Blind as a bat.

The Free Fall (3/18/2020)
(Stock market crashes and collapses)

Drop, drop, circuit breaker halts the free fall.
All indices racing down at a record speed.
Big, small, no fish break away from the trawl.

Heaven to underworld, you have seen it all;
up, down, zig, zag, dead cat's bounce, fear and greed.
Drop, drop, circuit breaker halts the free fall.

Odysseus reached kingdom of the dead, land of soul.
Showed him the path to go home, Tiresias never lied.
Big, small, no fish break away from the trawl.

Aeneas entered hell, what a grisly brawl.
Rome would be born, Anchises affirmed a new breed.
Drop, drop, circuit breaker halts the free fall.

Puts, calls, out of options, pray for the Call.
God bless America, please stop the bleed.
Big, small, no fish break away from the trawl.

Odysseus fished a way out to go home.
Aeneas's descendants found the empire of Rome.
Today, how do we stop the drop, halt the freefall?
Big, small, no fish break away from the trawl.

Nature's Rule (3/19/2020)
(Inspired by a poem of Holy Father Pope Francis)

Prayer is a sign, alone, we are not.
Problems are a hint that we are strong.
Pain means you are alive, nothing clots.

Wind enjoys not sailing, but it pilots the yacht.
River drinks no water while bird sings song.
Prayer is a sign, alone, we are not.

You eat fruit from trees and build a cot.
Thunderous lightning bolt strikes a gong.
Pain means you are alive nothing clots.

Sun does not shine on itself, turns cold to hot.
John wasn't worthy to untie His sandal's thong.
Prayer is a sign, alone, we are not.

Flowers spread their fragrance is not a plot,
not for themselves, but Designed for the throng.
Pain means you are alive, nothing clots.

The masses are happy because of you, a new lot;
live for others, nature's rule, it's been there all along.
Prayer is a sign, alone, we are not.
Pain means you are alive, nothing clots.

Shelter in Place (3/20/2020)

A new way of life, shelter in place.
Stay at home, now an order, a new rule.
The invisible enemy in our face.

Once, Paris robbed and took Helen to his place.
Greeks were all out to fight Trojans to bring her back.
Gods, goddesses, imposed from a distance.

And now, homebound to save lives, keep our grace.
Do not wander around, don't be a fool.
The invisible enemy in our face.

Aeneas stole Dido's heart, duty-bound his chase,
sailed to Italy, filled his mission in full.
Gods, goddesses, imposed from a distance.

It has arrived, sail, no sail; chase or no chase.
Sun still shines, but only ducklings in the pool.
The invisible enemy in our face.

How to hold our bearing? Even just a trace.
Close, shut down, all shopping malls, every school.
Gods, goddesses, imposed from a distance.
The invisible enemy in our face.

Two Weeks Ago (3/21/2020)

Two weeks ago, sun was bright, sky was blue.
Beach, street, cafe, bar: chat, laugh, buzz in the air.
Now, setback, panic, fear, it isn't just the flu.

Retreated to the shore, Agamemnon and every crew.
Fighting against Hector, no one dared.
Two weeks ago, sun was bright, sky was blue.

Ships in flames, up to their necks in slough.
Patroclus waged war, rose from Achilles' lair.
Charged, charged, fired up every crew.

In Achilles' armor, Patroclus sparked the coup.
Hector killed Patroclus, smothered the flare.
Two weeks ago, sun was bright, sky was blue.

A new shield for Achilles, like a lion, he slew
Hector, and every Trojan he stared.
Charged, charged, fired up every crew.

In weeks, after ten years, Priam slain; Troy was through.
What epoch? Now, how we miss noises, hugs and care?
Two weeks ago, sun was bright, sky was blue.
Beach, street, café, bar, we laugh, we buzz.

Shakespeare's Lockdown (3/22/2020)

Cases shoot up, market dives, frighten and scare.
Is the ship sailing to a cove or a shipwreck?
All isolated, kneeling in prayer.

"plagues that hang in this pendulous air."
Shakespeare wrote "King Lear" during the plague.
Cases shoot up, market dives, frighten and scare.

"The dead man's knell," "scarce asked for who,"
A speech in "Macbeth," crowd taken aback.
All isolated, kneeling in prayer.

"before the flowers in their caps dying or ere
they sicken." "good men's lives expire" the speech smack.
Cases shoot up, market dives, frighten and scare.

Theater shut down, he turned to poetry, same flair.
"Venus and Adonis," never a minute wasted.
All isolated, kneeling in prayer.

Quarantine or not, he shined and blared.
Plague, pestilence; plays, poems to fill the slack.
Cases shoot up, market dives, frighten and scare.
All isolated, kneeling in prayer.

II
I Can See It in My Daughters' Eyes

How to See the Light (3/23/2020)

Now, the daily news is so dismal, so drear.
How to cheer up? How to see the light?
The spirits are so haggard, so sere.

Once Titanic set sail, skies blue, ocean clear.
Admiration, acclaim, hubris reached its height.
The whole world awed and cheered.

The White Star of unsinkable ships without peer,
hit the iceberg, ignited the panic of their plight.
The spirits are so haggard, so sere.

Warnings abound, Thrinacia island, don't come near.
Curse, prophecy; stay away from that site.
The crew didn't listen, they were so tired.

Circe, Tiresias couldn't stop them going there.
Odysseus' men killed Helios' cattle, what a sin!
The spirits are so haggard, so sere.

Titanic folded its voyage, price paid, so dear.
Odysseus' men paid no heed, a blow outright.
Once the whole world awed and cheered.
Now, the spirits are so haggard, so sere.

Persephone's Regret (3/24/2020)

Ongoing debate, cease lockdown? A quick end?
Or longer span: GDP? Human lives? Bet on which side?
Ignore piling corpses, dine out and spend?

Where's the sun? Persephone's heart torn and rent.
Hades abducted and made her his bride.
A long lockdown or a quick end?

Demeter asked for help, summoned every friend.
"Going home," is Persephone's dream,
"Out of underworld" is her reverie.

Deal done, if ate nothing there, she can wend
homeward from hell to restore her pride.
A long lockdown or a quick end?

49

Hades snuck a seed in her mouth, she ate.
A fatal blunder, let guard down, she rued and cried.
Now, if ignored piling corpses, will we regret?

A grave sin, dead bodies on the street, no words can mend.
Ignore piling corpses, dine out and spend?
In hell, she grieved, sighed, tears ran dry.
Where's the sun? Persephone's heart torn and rent.

They All Die Alone (3/25/2020)

Priests administer last rites over the phone,
while families sit somberly at home.
At the end, lonely death, they all die alone.

At the bedsides, no one sobs, no one mourns.
A routine process, let the souls roam.
Priests administer last rites over the phone.

A place near the first circle of inferno
for these souls, Dante shall enact a new dome.
At the end, lonely death, they all die alone.

Await the final hugs and words, freeze in the zone.
Between heaven and hell, float like foam.
Priests administer last rites over the phone.

No chance to say goodbyes, hearts are torn.
No funerals, no closures, out of norm.
At the end, lonely death, they all die alone.

Lost, gone, vanished in the perfect storm?
Next to Limbo, waiting for the call.
Priests administer last rites over the phone.
At the end, lonely death, they all die alone.

Odysseus Hunkers Down (3/26/2020)

Pause, reopen; breath, tomb; alive or dough.
How to navigate? A pivotal call.
Life, death, a reality, not a reality show.

Scylla? Charybdis? Bear which blow?
Odysseus cramp his flair, not to fight at all.
Pause, reopen; breath, tomb; alive or dough.

Hunker down, Odysseus' men row, row, row.
Shirk Charybdis' whirlpool, surging breakers and fall.
Scylla? Charybdis? Bear which blow?

Six hideous heads, swaying necks to behold, a throe.
Scylla snatched six men; shriek, wail and bawl.
Pause, reopen; breath, tomb; alive or dough.

In Scylla's cave, writhing, choking, grisly woe.
Devouring the sea, spewed it up, Charybdis's trawl.
Scylla? Charybdis? Bear which blow?

Don't plunge us into ruin, helmsman, steer the oar.
Put clashing rocks astern, free us from this thrall.
Pause, reopen; breath, tomb; alive or dough.
Scylla? Charybdis? Bear which blow?

Who Is Fighting the War (3/27/2020)

It's a war, it's a war, every minute people die.
Piling corpses, deserted souls, mounting death tolls.
Who is fighting the war, holding our sky?

No fighter planes, no naval ships, a new outcry.
No soldiers, no guns, no tanks.
It's a war, it's a war, every minute people die.

Bullets, no, bombing, no; enemy is nigh.
No drones, no missiles, no nukes.
Who is fighting the war? Holding our sky?

Nurses, doctors on the frontline, scientists pry.
"We shall fight on the beaches,"* hills, fields, tap all holes.
It's a war, it's a war, every minute people die.

Store clerks, warehouse workers, delivery guys.
Grocery, pharmacy, hospitals, vital roles.
Who is fighting the war? Holding our sky?

Invisible enemy grows, doubles, multiplies.
There's no choice, we must fight back as a whole.
It's a war, it's a war, every minute people die.
Who is fighting the war? Holding our sky?

*Winston Church's speech during World War II.

I Can See It in My Daughters' Eyes (3/28/20)
(Inspired by governor Andrew Cuomo's daily briefing on 3/27/2020)

"I can see it in my daughters' eyes,
when I talk to them about this every night.
I can see the fear....they're taking it all in."*

This will transform how we think and what we are.
It'll form a new generation through this blight.
I can see it in my daughters' eyes.

No one is alone, regardless the color of skin.
No one's been here before; we're all in, in this fight.
I can see the fear...they're taking it all in.

It'll change us; how we live, how we buy,
how we work, how we stand up against this fright.
I can see it in my daughters' eyes.

Loved ones die, supplies are running thin,
it's heartbreaking to witness this plight.
I can see the fear....they're taking it all in.

They won't remember who lost or who won.
They'll remember who saved lives, turned on the light.
I can see it in my daughters' eyes.
I can see the fear...they're taking it all in.

*Governor Andrew Cuomo's daily briefing on 3/27/2020,
reported in the Los Angeles Times by Seema Mehta and
Melanie Mason on the same day.

It Is Coming (3/29/2020)

You can hear it, around the world, day and night.
It's near, how dire, no one can pay no heed.
What to do? No place to hide, no end in sight.

Swine fever killed all hogs, a graver plight.
Circe's potion is not what we need.
You can hear it, around the world, day and night.

Death all over, bubonic plague, a horrible blight.
Shakespeare's time, poetry, play, a different breed.
What to do? No place to hide, no end in sight.

You wake up, you breathe, you're blessed.
One day at a time, give us our daily bread.
You can hear it around the world, day and night.

Vaccine, the only cure, the white knight.
Tips, advice, don't spread, don't mislead.
What to do? No place to hide, no end in sight.

Pray sky won't fall, pray there is still light.
Please, have mercy on us, listen to our plea.
You can hear it around the world, day and night.
What to do? No place to hide, no end in sight.

III
She Is Coming

Edge of Doom (3/30/2020)

"Love alters not with his brief hours and weeks,
But bears it out even to the edge of doom."*
Time comes, all silent, not a single soul speaks.

The world comes to a halt with no squeaks.
All of a sudden, news is nothing but gloom.
"Love alters not with his brief hours and weeks."*

Is it a warning? The outlook is bleak.
Is it a sign? The unending battles loom.
Time comes, all silent, not a single soul speaks.

Are we losing the war? Kneel to the plague.
Over the phone, says goodbye, loved ones gone.
"Love alters not with his brief hours and weeks."*

Is it a lesson? Streets are bare and blank.
Refuge, shelter, who's next? For whom the bells mourn.
Time comes, all silent, not a single soul speaks.

Is it a punishment? Whole systems crack.
Listen, hurry, before all are torn.
"Love alters not with his brief hours and weeks."*
Time comes, all silent, not a single soul speaks.

*Shakespeare sonnet 116.

New York Siren's Shimmering in the Foggy Sky (3/31/2020); (Flashing white, warm red light at the top of Empire State Building to honor the emergency workers)

New York siren's shimmering in the foggy sky.
Empire State Building stays up throughout the night.
All night long, ambulances, trucks, wail and cry.

The soul is soaked with tears from red eyes.
The heart is beating with flashing white light.
New York siren's shimmering in the foggy sky.

Doctors, nurses, medical workers, our frontline.
New York is bleeding, a horrid sight.
All night long, ambulances, trucks, wail and cry.

Central Park into field hospital in no time.
The lungs of the city, its breath's getting tight.
New York siren's shimmering in the foggy sky.

USNS Comfort is coming to town, spirit's high.
A relief, navy hospital ship joins the fight.
All night long, ambulances, trucks, wail and cry.

Scores of medical volunteers answer the call.
Red, white, Empire State, a lighthouse through this blight.
New York siren's shimmering in the foggy sky.
All night long, ambulances, trucks, wail and cry.

She Is Coming (4/1/2020)

She is coming, she brings a glimmer of hope.
CSNS Comfort, meets the challenges of our time.
New York is almost at the end of its rope.

You can spot her with a flag in white coat.
Ready for rescue mission in any clime.
She is coming, she brings a glimmer of hope.

A relief for workers; loads are up to their throats.
It is a battle, an uphill climb.
New York is almost at the end of its rope.

She sails by Lady Liberty's wide scope,
Coast Guard helicopter flies above; sky is blue.
She is coming, she brings a glimmer of hope.

She sails up the Hudson, escorted by tug boats.
A glimpse of light, a moment so true.
New York is almost at the end of its rope.

Emotion, struggle; how we fight, how we cope.
A pledge, a determination, every crew.
She is coming, she brings a glimmer of hope.
New York is almost at the end of its rope.

A Seven Week Lockdown (4/2/2020)
(Seven Weeks, *3/16/20 to 5/3/20*)

Over the cliff, Odysseus sobs and groans,
wrenching his heart, gazing beyond barren sea.
Longing to go home, pining to the bone.

Seven years, Calypso island; tears, moans,
sunrise, sunset; crave, yearn, no one hears his plea.
Over the cliff, Odysseus sobs and groans.

Lotus-eaters, Cyclops, Aeolus after Cicones.
Scylla, Charybdis, sun god's ire, as Circe foresees.
Longing to go home, pining to the bone.

After Trojan War, Odysseus led the fleet home.
A general, an admiral; now, a single soul.
Over the cliff, Odysseus sobs and groans.

A plot to kill his son, as Odysseus roams.
Telemachus in danger, Penelope in the hole.
Longing to go home, pining to the bone.

Seven years, life is but a dream of foam.
Seven weeks, world is paying an immense toll.
Over the cliff, Odysseus sobs and groans.
Longing to go home, pining to the bone.

What Message for the Day? (4/3/2020)

Is that You? Sending Hermès through heaven's grey,
"plunged to the sea, skimmed the waves like a tern."*
Down from Pieria, what message for the day?

"No one listen, so seize the world, shelter and stay."
Now we are all ears, we got no place to turn.
Is that You? Sending Hermès through heaven's grey.

Fever like fires on earth, all astray,
cough like pollutants clot the throat.
Down from Pieria, what message for the day?

Submerged as sea inches up to flood coast and bay.
No touches, no hugs, short breath to death, countless slain.
Is that You? Sending Hermès through heaven's grey.

Would you think of humans and earth when you pray?
Thrash insidious virus, please stop the pain.
Down from Pieria, what message for the day?

Wars, fights, land grabs, continue to battle and fray.
Wake up, wake up, before Hermès comes again.
Is that You? Sending Hermès through heaven's grey.
Down from Pieria, what message for the day?

*"The Odyssey" translated by Robert Fagles.

No One's Awake Even After Rooster's Crow (4/4/2020)

How did it all start? And when did we know?
"History does not repeat itself, but it rhymes."*
No one's awake even after rooster's crow.

No one can see, they just hide and grow.
Kill, kill, silent killers, crime or no crime.
How did it all start? And when did we know?

Forlorn horn-sounds, foreboding a grievous blow.
Paul Revere's riding against time.
No one's awake even after rooster's crow.

No mercy, no one can escape, ally or foe.
Under fire, the old, the young in their prime.
How did it all start? And when did we know?

Rotten pith and trunk, spoiled sprig and bough.
All in a flash, only wish it's a farce, a mime.
No one's awake even after rooster's crow.

First to go, elders grind through the death throes.
Distress, desolate, corpses, hellholes, filth and grime.
How did it all start? And when did we know?
No one's awake even after rooster's crow.

*A quote from Mark Twain.

What Do We Know? (4/5/2020)

What do we know? Are you sure? Is that true?
So many whizzes and tips pop up in my email.
Let me know, when will all this be through?

Will we return to normal life, any clue?
Just wait for the vaccine, but could it not fail?
What do we know? Are you sure? Is that true?

The virus attacked all, regardless who is who,
a guessing game, it may end with another tale.
Let me know, when will all this be through?

After the war, Odysseus led the fleet and crew
to go home; couple months if it's a smooth sail.
But what do we know? Are you sure? Is that true?

It took Odysseus a decade, everybody knew.
A few months' voyage became a ten-year ordeal.
Let me know, when will all this be through?

We don't know what we don't know, is the only truth
until we find coronavirus's Achilles' heel.
But what do we know? Are you sure? Is that true?
Let me know, when will all this be through?

IV
Sea to Shining Sea

April Rain, April Fog (4/6/2020)

April rain, April fog, cloud and cover all,
cloak the entire valley, nuzzle window panes.
Every creation is standing still like a wall.

Budding sprig, fresh new leaves hidden in the veil.
The foggy blur discloses another empty day.
April rain, April fog, cloud and cover all.

Trails next to barn, streets near town, the whole dale
muffled in the quiet brume, minding their own ways.
Every creation is standing still like a wall.

A drizzling morning, now a heavy rainfall.
Raindrops beat the panes, shrieking in pain.
April rain, April fog, cloud and cover all.

A peek of sunlight, a rainbow after the downpour
unveils flowering cherries, plums: red, white and pink.
Every creation is standing still like a wall.

Clean stones, benches, asphalt near the town hall.
Bright buds cradled in the branches, glitter and blink.
April rain, April fog, cloud and cover all.
Every creation is standing still like a wall.

The Evil Stops Not to Profit From This Blow
(4/7/2020)

Pharaoh refuses to let the people go.
The Lord struck down, plague after plague.
The evil stops not to profit from this blow.

Water becomes blood, frogs jump and crawl.
His heart hardened right after he implored and begged,
Pharaoh refuses to let the people go.

Gnats, flies, livestock, boils, what else to know?
Easily seen, readily visible, signs are not vague.
The evil stops not to profit from this blow.

Hail, locusts, darkness, suffering and woe.
No changes, while everyone is crazed and mad.
Pharaoh refuses to let the people go.

The plague on firstborn; a true despair and throe.
First son of pharaoh, slave girl.... baby or lad.
The evil stops not to profit from this blow.

Today, end to end on earth, a ghastly toll.
It is beyond what words can say; dire, sad.
Pharaoh refuses to let the people go.
The evil stops not to profit from this blow.

Yesterday Is the Longest Sunny Day. (4/8/2020)

Yesterday is the longest sunny day.
It shines, refuses darkness, sun is sanity.
After rains, skies refresh, bounce ray by ray.

Do not greet, do not open mouth, do not say.
We know what's in thin air, witness the crudity.
Yesterday is the longest sunny day.

A sin? God's disfavor has a role to play?
Who offended? Why do innocents pay the penalty?
After rains, skies refresh, bounce ray by ray.

Apollo sent a plague, spread and slay
the Greeks. Calchas deciphers with clarity.
Yesterday is the longest sunny day.

That plague ended in weeks; today's virus stays.
Does it humble us? A blow to our bigotry.
After rains, skies refresh, bounce ray by ray.

Empty streets, coyotes prowl in search of prey.
Bounded home, ponder we, eternal verity?
Yesterday is the longest sunny day.
After rains, skies refresh, bounce ray by ray.

Is the Time Near? (4/9/2020)

"Let him who is vile continue to be vile;
Let him who does right continue to do right."*
Is the time near? The judgement? The trial?

The end game? Triggers meeting guile with guile?
Roaming on bare streets? Hiding in fright?
"Let him who is vile continue to be vile;"

Shelter in place, stay home, enclaved on an isle.
The daily rituals transform into a rite.
Is the time near? The judgement? The trial?

"Exodus" to "Revelation," the riles;
the ten plagues, seven plagues; beginning to end.
"Let him who is vile continue to be vile;"

Hoarding, fraud, gouging, ripoff, wile to wile;
Smear, lie, swindle, bogus, black becomes white.
Is the time near? The judgement? The trial?

Pestilence muted human's rancor and bile.
For a moment, do tears shed a glimmer of light?
"Let him who is vile continue to be vile;"
Is the time near? The judgement? The trial?

*"Revelation" book 22:11

Today Is a Holy Friday (4/10/2020, Good Friday)
(As of today, half of the world's population remains on lockdown)

"Raindrops on roses"* things I can see.
"Whiskers on kittens"* things I can feel.
Think of good things, be happy as you can be.

Today is Good Friday, goodness conquered sin.
Scars may remain, wounds inflicted will heal.
"Raindrops on roses"* things I can see.

A holy day; love defeats hate, love always wins.
An austere day, silent are our church bells.
Think of good things, be happy as you can be.

A somber day, listen to the plea.
A bleak day, penance in the solitude of cell.
"Raindrops on roses"* things I can see.

From darkness to joy, set our souls free.
Suffering, sacrifice, heaven and hell.
Think of good things, be happy as you can be.

"My Favorite Things" Julie Andrews sings.
Let us echo, we'll live well, let us yell.
"Raindrops on roses"* things I can see.
Think of good things, be happy as you can be.

*Lyrics of song "My Favorite Things" (From movie "Sound of Music.")

Not to Yield (4/11/20, Saturday)
(The Global Death Toll Over 100,000; Paschal Triduum 2020
began in the evening of Thursday, April 9, and ends in the
evening of Sunday, April 12);

Crucified, in the tomb; would the wounds be healed?
Death toll over hundred thousand; the world mourns.
"To strive, to seek, to find, and not to yield."*

Are there any means, weapons left to wield?
No hugs, no kisses, no goodbyes, the world torn.
Crucified, in the tomb; would the wounds be healed?

Carry on, fight, fight back, where is Achilles' shield?
Before the waves, gulfs slam us, all drown.
"To strive, to seek, to find, and not to yield."*

One by one, high, low, homeless, best-heeled.
None are spared, every country, every town.
Crucified, in the tomb; would the wounds be healed?

Holy Saturday, a stillness to all wheeled.
For a day, in hell, we pause, all die down.
"To strive, to seek, to find, and not to yield."*

Scientists, every corner of medical field,
dig, dig, test, test; new, old, lone and lorn.
Crucified, in the tomb; would the wounds be healed?
"To strive, to see, to find, and not to yield."*

*From the poem "Ulysses" written in 1842 by Alfred, Lord
Tennyson.

Sea to Shining Sea
(4/12/2020, Easter Sunday)
(U.S. Death Toll Over 20,000)

"A voice in the darkness, a knock at the door."*
From coast to coast, sea to shining sea.
"And a word that shall echo forevermore,"*

A strike, a lightening down to the core.
Resurrected from the dead; we are on our knees.
"A voice in the darkness, a knock at the door."*

Bore the fate of a nation, he rode and roared;
a cry of alarm: "Wake up, wake up and see."
"And a word that shall echo forevermore."*

Enemy already landed at the shore,
wave after wave, gathered around the quay.
"A voice in the darkness, a knock at the door."*

Crisis? Turning point? A mortal pledge in store.
Clock is ticking; can you hear the uproar and plea?
"And a word that shall echo forevermore."*

Place our trust in the hands of almighty Lord.
Implore forgiveness, forgive our sins.
"A voice in the darkness, a knock at the door."*
"And a word that shall echo forevermore."*

*From the poem "Paul Revere's Ride" by Henry Wadsworth
Longfellow.

V
I Will Arise and Go Now

We Will Meet Again (4/13/2020)
(U.K. Death Toll Over 10,000)

"With his nostrils like pits full of blood to the brim,"*
Twilight, moonlight, midnight, sunlight, galloping through.
"And with circles of red for his eye-sockets' rim."*

Good news? No one knows. Or could it be grim?
All we know, it's life or death, it's overdue.
"With his nostrils like pits full of blood to the brim."*

Queen, 93, her speech ends with "We will meet again."**
"We will succeed,"** she knows so well, she knew.
"And with circles of red for his eye-sockets' rim."*

"We'll be with our families and friends again,
while we may have more still to endure."**
"With his nostrils like pits full of blood to the brim."*

101

A shimmer is hope regardless how dim.
It will come if you believe it is true.
"And with circles of red for his eye-sockets' rim."*

Don't know when or where, but we'll meet again.
"Better days will return,"** we'll start anew.
"With his nostrils like pits full of blood to the brim."*
"And with circles of red for his eye-sockets' rim."*

*From the poem "How They Brought the Good News from Ghent to Aix" written in 1845 by Robert Browning.
**Queen Elizabeth's coronavirus speech on 4/5/2020.

A Gulf Apart, so Far, so Nigh (4/14/2020)

(President Donald Trump and New York Governor Andrew
Cuomo clashed over who has more power to reopen the
economy.)

"and I, I took the one less traveled by,"*
alone, day after day, tread a dirt path.
No one to say hi or bye.

Who has the right to decide who lives or dies?
Politics? Science? Up to the stats or math?
"and I, I took the one less traveled by,"*

A gulf apart, so far, so nigh.
Tempers flare, outbursts of wrath.
No one to say hi or bye.

It's not a time to lament or sigh.
Where are the plans and pith?
"and I, I took the one less traveled by,"*

How do we stop all the dying and outcries?
Isn't this the crux?
No one to say hi or bye.

Who calls the shots? Whose lives on the line?
Your call or mine? Or Virus's?
"and I, I took the one less traveled by,"*
No one to say hi or bye.

*From the poem "The Road Not Taken" written in 1916 by
Robert Frost.

Five Stages of Grief (4/15/2020)
(Denial, anger, bargaining, depression and acceptance)*

Loved ones, jobs; how to accept all losses, tell me how.
Ignoring relief station and breadline.
Did Grief pass the denial stage in his vow?

Real issues of depression lingering on,
country was lost, no empathy, no spine.
How do we accept all losses, tell me how?

Denial, anger, bargain; let bygones be gone.
Depress, accept; let the truth talk, no whine.
Did Grief pass the denial stage in his vow?

Rivals flare up; bickering pro and con.
The lies and cover-ups distort the clear sign.
How do we accept all losses, tell me how?

Staggering evidence, time to act is now.
Seething animus boils against the crime.
Did Grief pass the denial stage in his vow?

Depravity, greed, through years of sowing and plow.
Rip-off, defraud; poor and have-nots in the grime.
Loved ones, jobs; how to accept all losses, tell me how.
Did Grief pass the denial stage in his vow?

*Elisabeth Kubler-Ross model

Rainy Days? (4/16/2020)

It was yesterday, winds blew from the west,
behind our wings, kept us in the race.
Pulsing, pursuing, where is my nest?

Aeolus captured all winds, granted Odysseus's quest;
homebound, only west winds left to pace.
Pulsing, pursuing, where is his nest?

Unleashed the squalls, surprised and vexed,
sack opened, a lapse threw them back into a mess.
It was yesterday, winds blew from the west.

This time, Aeolus refused to help, no more yes.
Odysseus abashed and perplexed.
Pulsing, pursuing, where is his nest?

Once it was in harmony, all the best.
Now, sickness, death, loss, no one at peace.
It was yesterday, winds blew from the west.

Swagger, twerk like no tomorrow, the young were blessed.
Rainy days? Nay. Now virus is a lifetime witness.
Pulsing, pursuing, where is my nest?
It was yesterday, winds blew from the west.

I Measure the Sunset With Steps I Take
(4/17/2020)
(For Theodore Roethke)

I sleep and wake, wake and sleep and wake.
I ponder things that most I fear.
I measure the sunset with steps I take.

I watch the moving clouds to claim their stake.
I know the rain will rain, the sky will clear.
I sleep and wake, wake and sleep and wake.

All I see, all I hear, I wish all were fake.
God's blessing, I witness wild flowers blooming near.
I measure the sunset with steps I take.

I count the hues and layers before daybreak.
Bouncing the sprigs, birds still chirp in the air.
I sleep and wake, wake and sleep and wake.

You said, there are ways to shake this ache.
The lonely deer finds her home through roam and veer.
I measure the sunset with steps I take.

I number and fathom the days yet to make.
Losses, drear, hold tight to something dear.
I sleep and wake, wake and sleep and wake.
I measure the sunset with steps I take.

Find Your Peace Into That Goodnight (4/18/20)

"Let there be light," and there was light.*
Stacking corpses, loading trucks, sack by sack.
Find your peace into that good night.

Everyone is in the same boat fighting this blight.
The world is in chaos, everything has a crack.**
"Let there be light," and there was light.*

Falling souls bewildered by the fatal bite.
Ferryman refused their coins, turned them back.
Find your peace into that good night.

Mom, dad, son, daughter....no time to say goodbye.
Floating souls in Limbo, squeeze and pack.
"Let there be light," and there was light.*

111

Pray for angels to come, see the grisly sight.
The world is being ruined by wildfire of plague.
Find your peace into that good night.

Wrath, ire, set aside, the end is not nigh.
Tears, resolve, keep going before the shipwreck.
"Let there be light," and there was light.
Find your peace into that good night.

*Genesis, 1:3
**Leonard Cohen, "There is a crack in everything, that's how the light gets in."

I Will Arise and Go Now (4/19/2020)
Inspired by the poem "The Lake Isle of Innisfree" written in 1890 by W. B. Yeats.

I will arise and go to Bar Harbor, Maine.
Be a butterfly dancing in the sun.
I will go now, break the humdrum and mundane.

A squirrel spurs for blueberries on the plain.
A skunk in the holes between rocks, bide and stun.
I will arise and go to Bar Harbor, Maine.

Be a chipmunk, foraging for insects and worms,
a bald eagle extends his wings, covers the sky.
I will go now, break the humdrum and mundane.

A seagull circles the beach, patrols his reign.
A starfish in the tide pool, swims for fun.
I will arise and go to Bar Harbor, Maine.

When tides fall, I will go slow, breezes ease and wane,
sail boat fading, my mind no longer on the run.
I will go now, break the humdrum and mundane.

Learn from hermit crab how to conceal and feign,
be a hummingbird, look busy, nothing done.
I will arise and go to Bar Harbor, Maine.
I will go now, break the humdrum and mundane.

VI
What Do I Do If You Fall?

I Don't Know Why (4/20/2020)
(for Pablo Neruda)

I don't know why it came in search of me.
I don't know when or how it came.
It came in the light or dark, I couldn't see.

Dust in the wind, breezes rustle in the tree.
A speck in the universe, it has no name.
I don't know why it came in search of me.

It sails in a canoe on the wild sea,
in and out of waves, don't know where to aim.
It came in the light or dark, I couldn't see.

I know it is there, still coming, it seems.
Nothing to hook on, nothing to claim.
I don't know why it came in search of me.

A small bird, a nest, it's real, not a dream.
It's neither words nor voices, it is calm.
It came in the light or dark, I couldn't see.

It is not a summons, it carries no theme.
It was cold, I can feel it now, it is warm.
I don't know why it came in search of me.
It came in the light or dark, I couldn't see.

Maybe a Crack or a Hole? (4/21/2020)

And it touched me on my face, in my soul.
Could it be a feather? I was blind, my mouth dry.
Through the wall, maybe a crack or a hole?

I just followed, grabbed the wings, swung and strolled.
It was blurred, I tried to open my eyes.
And it touched me on my face, in my soul.

Pulsed with bits and shreds, I retreated from any role,
my soul rambles, gropes, for a place to hide.
Through the wall, maybe a crack or a hole?

Lingered behind, something popped, a word,
or two, it began to form a line in my mind.
And it touched me on my face, in my soul.

When it started, it waged from head to toe,
a wave raged, landed, continued as trickle and tide.
Through the wall, maybe a crack or a hole?

It came in many modes; warm and cold.
It silenced all the probes and pries.
And it touched me on my face, in my soul.
Through the wall, maybe a crack or a hole?

Never Happened Before (4/22/2020)
(The U.S. benchmark crude for May delivery fell Monday
(4/21/2020) to a settlement price of minus $37.63 per
barrel.)

Fall, fall, fall, oil prices fall.
Price turns negative, never happened before.
The world grinds to a halt.

They pay you, just haul away; please just haul.
Sky is the limit, zero is not the floor.
Fall, fall, fall, oil prices fall.

A dystopian jungle? Who is pumping gas?
Glut, deluge, rip common sense, cut to the core.
The world grinds to a halt.

Guru, pro, trader, folks, every class.
Tears, blood, so sore; only solace, not just you
Fall, fall, fall, oil prices fall.

Bankrupt, ruined, a calculated brawl.
Wipe out competitors, it is a war.
The world grinds to a halt.

What comes next? Who dares to guess?
Not a fragment of armor remains.
Fall, fall, fall, oil prices fall.
The world grinds to a halt.

How Long? But How? (4/23/2020)

The old think how not to die.
Stay at home, shelter in place, how long? But how?
The young worry how to live.

Nursing home, where is home? How to say goodbye?
Poor immune system, first to go, they know.
The old think how not to die.

The young want parties, bars, cafes, beaches; fly, drive,
climb mountains, dive any ocean, live high, not low.
The young worry how to live.

The world stops, the threat and death are nigh.
They're old, seen enough, not this one, such throe.
The old think how not to die.

Prom, graduation, year after year, compete, strive;
in a flash, the dream all shattered now.
The young worry how to live.

Parched ground, grim drought, ask the barren blue, why?
And where? A drop of rain, a word of relief?
The old think how not to die.
The young worry how to live.

It Keeps Us Waiting in the Dark (4/24/2020)
(U.S. death toll over 50,000, death toll crested over 20,000 on 4/12/2020)

And it keeps us waiting in the dark.
But in broad daylight, sun gazes at the sky.
No wind needed to fan the embers, ignites spark.

Deafening silence, no one minds, no dogs bark.
Numb is the norm, everyday people die.
And it keeps us waiting in the dark.

In the ocean, there are still whale and shark.
Up in the blue, hardly see any planes fly.
No wind needed to fan the embers, ignites spark.

Wheel turns, clock ticks, today, another landmark.
It comes and goes, nothing rattles, tears run dry.
And it keeps us waiting in the dark.

Who cares how many days Noah was in the ark.
Is fifty thousand deaths just a number, a sigh?
No wind needed to fan the embers, ignites spark.

Once, bumper to bumper, Disneyland park.
Now, line is longer to food bank, in our eyes.
And it keeps us waiting in the dark.
No wind needed to fan the embers, ignites spark.

An Uproar in Slow Motion *(4/25/2020)*

When sad and ill what do I do?
I wish clock is dead, stop the bleed,
and a rope to lift me out of blue.

When up and high, everything looks new,
I wish clock is dead, time freezes and heeds,
in a flash it fades like morning dew.

And now, world hits the wall, petrified in glue.
Breathe and eat, that is all I can need.
No rope to lift me out of blue.

A vicious invisible coup,
an uproar in slow motion with grinding speed.
It may pass, it may come back from what we knew.

A new world is waiting when this is through.
Count the pieces we cede.
Pick up the rest, drop the ruse.

When will that be? Isn't it overdue?
Or never be? Regardless the plea,
Why? What? When? Where? How to get to the end?
A new world is waiting when this is through.

What Do I Do If You Fall? (4/26/2020)

What do I do if you fall?
Where can I go?
Who to call?

The night will be cold.
How to keep the kitchen flow?
What do I do if you fall?

The world will be on hold.
When everything is slow,
who to call?

Who to share when kids grow tall?
And the jokes, stories, I know.
What do I do if you fall?

And with whom to grow old?
Thumb through album, all those joys and woes,
who to share, who to call?

Where will the soul rest before it folds,
sunrise, sunset, to and fro?
What do I do if you fall?
Who to share, who to call?

VII
Will I Hear It?

Where Is Home? (4/27/2020)

No place to go?
Birds fly,
sky is their home.

Termites never stop digging underground home.
Red-headed hummingbird, so frenzied in our eyes.
Dante dredged, deepened nine circles tomb.

Stuck at home.
Same room, same window, same sky.
Rattlesnakes roam.

Butterflies cruise and glow.
Coyotes prowl and pry.
Poke, nag, woodpecker's dins grow.

River continues its flow.
Mountain is standing by.
Is it still the time to plant and sow?

The world suffers a heavy blow.
Men cry and die.
No place to go.
Where is home?

Mirror (4/28/2020)

Mirror, mirror on the wall.
Ugly, pretty, evil, moral, true or fraud.
Who knows what is the next call?

Snow White was the fairest of all,
jealous queen made her flee and bawl.
Mirror, mirror on the wall.

Aphrodite won the brawl.
Helen was Paris's reward.
Trojan War, the next call.

And now, the invisible virus on the wall.
It reflects the wicked who sin and hoard,
lights up the front lines who stand tall.

It illuminates the able, Elba; rise and fall;
magnifies whose acumen strikes the chord.
Mirror, mirror on the wall.

Apathy, empathy, it shines them all.
It spotlights who stands out, who's backward.
Mirror, mirror on the wall.
Who knows what is the next call?

I Hear the Winds Moan (4/29/2020)
(for Derek Walcott)

I want to be the tussock sedge in the bog,
sway my head as breezes blow,
dance with my dear jumping frogs.

I want to be the release dove,
open a ceremony, salute a milestone,
witness the harmony of peace and love.

Yet, I stay home, shut the door, live my life.
Here, fake news, lies; I hear the winds moan.
What will battlefield look like after this strife?

I want to hear the haunting call,
when common loons lament their woes,
echo forsaken dreams of lingering goals.

I want to see flamingo at the zoo,
ask her how to take a bow,
and ask white egret how not to regret.

I want to be the tussock sedge in the bog,
dance with my dear jumping frogs.
I want to be the release dove,
witness the harmony of peace and love.

Persephone's Spring (4/30/2020)

Day after day,
laughter in the dell,
Spring Maiden plays.

His heart of stone touched by her gaiety,
Hades heard it well.
Day after day.

Red, white, purple, yellow, no gray;
Wild roses, tall irises, bloom and smell.
Spring Maiden plays.

One day, Persephone strays,
earth splits, caught in Hades arms,
she shrieks and yells.
Sad, pale, thereafter, day by day.

Not Sherlock Holmes can find the needle in the hay,
nor can Edgar Allan Poe ring "The Bells."*
Spring Maiden no longer plays.

April is almost gone, it will soon be May.
Tell me,
when will you come back,
be freed from hell?
So again,
Spring Maiden plays
in the sun,
day after day.

*A poem by Edgar Allan Poe.

144

Let Us Pretend (5/1/2020)

let us pretend
nothing ever happened
we didn't all die at the end

we will reboot
clean all bugs
restart and reroute

for a second
back to 2019
let us pretend

hundreds on the platform
taking the same train
thousands at the concert

stadium packed
hot dogs, beer, peanuts
no sports? a sin, a plague

parties, birthdays
anniversaries
let us karaoke

let us all wear pink
for the second round
who will buy the drinks

hugs, kisses
hand in hand
#1 thing we miss

for a second
let us pretend

I Can See It With My Own Eye (5/2/2020)
(for Rabindranath Tagore)

I float my paper boat into the sky,
will winds carry the flight?
There's the address of the village I came from.

Caught by a stream, it flies,
buoys like a kite.
I can see it with my own eyes.

Miles, miles, it travels quiet and mum.
When you spot the boat, regardless how late,
tell me, tell me, I'll hear a distant drum.

Winds are howling through the strait.
Where are you in this stormy night?
Gust's pounding the gate of fate.

This morning, another cloudy day.
No one can see very far.
Every face tinted with grey.

Young and old, all the same,
waiting, waiting, day and night.
Miles, miles, it travels quiet and mum,
tell me, tell me, I'll hear a distant drum.

Will I Hear It? (5/3/2020)
(for Rabindranath Tagore)

I hear the step, no one comes,
maybe it's not for me.
All is silent, no one hums.

I hear the voice, no one sings,
it's dark, I can't see,
may be feather on the wings.

The lamp is not yet lit,
will he come? Through land or sea?
Will he knock? Will I hear it?

Is instrument strummed and in tune?
What chord? Which key?
Stars twinkle at the moon.

It is getting late.
Breezes still whisper in the trees.
It may be chilly, but I'll wait.

Will it shine and burn like a flame,
and finally, set us free?
I hear the voice, no one sings,
may be feather on the wings.

About the Author

This is Livingston Rossmoor's 17th book. As of 2020, he has written and published 14 poetry books. His poems have appeared in numerous publications: local newspapers, magazines, newsletters and overseas publications. In addition, Livingston's poems have been published in *Leaves-of-Ink*, *Poetry Quarterly, The Lyric* and *California Quarterly* (California State Poetry Society). He has also written 2 books of prose and poetry, 1 book of 13 short stories and composed 21 lyrics and melodies collected in 2 DVDs and 1 CD.

Over his 40 year career in publishing, Livingston oversaw the production of 12 printed consumer magazines. He formerly served as the editorial director of the journal: *Nourish-Poetry* and is currently an associate member of the Academy of American Poets and a member of the California State Poetry Society.

Livingston resides in California with his dear wife of 47 years. He has 3 children and 8 grandchildren.

EGW Publishing
(Since 1979)

www.egwpublishing.com
www.livingstonrossmoor.com

Made in the USA
Monee, IL
04 September 2020